594
CHA

Chambers, Catherine

Shells

Shells

Shells

CATHERINE CHAMBERS

RSVP

**RAINTREE
STECK-VAUGHN**
PUBLISHERS
The Steck-Vaughn Company

Austin, Texas

Published by Raintree Steck-Vaughn Publishers, an imprint of Steck-Vaughn Company

Library of Congress Cataloging-in-Publication Data
Chambers, Catherine.
    Shells / Catherine Chambers.
        p.   cm. — (Would you believe it!)
    Includes index.
    ISBN 0-8172-4101-9
    1. Shells — Miscellanea — Juvenile literature. [1. Shells.]
    I. Title. II. Series.
    QL405.2.C48   1996
    594'.0471 — dc20   95-22242
                                                                          CIP
                                                                          AC

Printed in Hong Kong
Bound in the United States
1 2 3 4 5 6 7 8 9 0 LB 99 98 97 96 95

Contents

What Is a Shell?

Seashells are the homes of soft sea creatures. Some shells are smaller than a grain of rice. Others are bigger than a kitchen sink! But all of them protect the animal's soft body that is inside. People find seashells very useful, too.

Starfish family
This sea urchin belongs to the starfish family. It has a hard shell underneath its long, prickly spines.

Tasty crustacea
This fierce-looking lobster is a member of the crustacea group of animals. Other members include crabs and shrimp.

Many mollusks
The pop-eyed squid (right) belongs to the large mollusk family. Unlike most other mollusks, its soft body is not protected by a shell. Clams, conchs, oysters, and mussels are all mollusks. So are scallops (below). Their shells grow from small glands that are on their bodies. These glands are like pouches.

Precious Shells

Shells can be rare and valuable. Some have been used as money. Other shells are treasured because they are connected with people's religious beliefs.

A sacred chank

This statue of the Indian Hindu god, Vishnu, is holding a rare, left-coiled chank shell. Indian Hindus believed Vishnu rescued their sacred writings, which had been stolen and hidden inside one of these shells.

The scallop of Saint James

You can see a carved scallop shell on this statue. It is the symbol of the Christian saint, James, who lived nearly 2,000 years ago. His body lies in the Spanish city of Santiago de Compostela. For hundreds of years, Christian pilgrims have walked from all over Europe to this holy place. Scallop-shell badges show others that they have completed the long journey.

Spending shells

Look at all of this money! Small cowrie shells were used as coins for many centuries. The ones shown here came from islands in the Pacific Ocean, 150 years ago. Cowrie coins were also used in West Africa.

Strings of shells

In the Solomon Islands of the Pacific Ocean, shells are broken and threaded onto string to be used as money. The shell money pictured below is part of a wedding gift.

Listening to Shells

Musical instruments can be made from shells! Some shells are huge tubes, like trumpets. Small, tough ones can rattle loudly when they are shaken.

Can you hear the ocean?

These are tiger cowries. Put one close to your ear. You will discover that the air inside of the hollow shape makes a sound like the ocean. People often use cowries to make rattles.

Shaking shells

These Mexican Indians are making music with a shell trumpet and with ankle rattles! The rattles are made from hundreds of clam shells. As the musicians dance and play, the shells shake with them.

Shell horns

Large shells are used as trumpets and horns all around the world, from Tibet to South America. This Peruvian Indian is using a conch shell as a horn.

Triton's trumpet

This huge shell is named after Triton, the god of the sea. He is always shown playing a shell horn. The musician here is blowing through a hole in the shell's side. He is calling to villagers on the Pacific island of Fiji.

Shell Shapes

The shape of some shells makes them useful as cups and bowls. Other shell shapes can be used to make long-lasting flower decorations.

Shell jugs

This bronze jug was made in Nigeria a thousand years ago. The makers copied the shape of a whelk shell. People also use real shells for carrying water.

Shell dishes

These scallop shells make very good plates. They are holding a meal, called Prawns of Saint James (see page 8).

Crab shells are also used as dishes. They can hold scooped-out crab meat, which is usually mixed with some kind of dressing or creamy sauce.

A shell font

This giant clam rests in a church on the Seychelle Islands of the Indian Ocean. New members of the Christian church are blessed with the water that is held in this shell.

Shapes made with shells

Would you believe that these flowers have been made with different kinds of shells? Many types of clam shells look like petals. The large, white flower in the middle is made of tellins, or sunset shells.

Showing Off Shells

Shells can be all sorts of colors. Some shells shine like silver on the inside. Others shine like rainbows. Shell decorations are used all over the world.

King Quetzalcoatl
The shell head of this Mexican Indian king is rising from a coyote's jaws! The head is thought to be from a palace entirely covered with shells that was built for Quetzalcoatl between the 7th and 9th century A.D.

Shell buttons
The buttons on this blanket are made of mother-of-pearl. This is the hard, shiny layer found inside of some mollusk shells. North American Indians made the blanket early this century.

Walls of shells

Thousands of shells have been set into the walls of this house on the west coast of England. Long, pointed augers make star shapes. Spiky spider conchs climb next to the steps. Scallop shells open out in a whirl of cowries.

A shell mask

This mask was made by the Bushoong people of Zaire, in Africa. It is covered with precious cowrie shells. The mask was used in a play performed only on royal occasions.

Shell Jewelry

One of the best ways to show off shells is to make jewelry from them. For thousands of years, people all over the world have made and worn shell jewelry.

Cutting shells

This woman is cutting shells to be made into jewelry. She is working in a factory in the Seychelle Islands. The islands have a good supply of shells from the Indian Ocean, which surrounds them.

Carving shells

Some shells can be carved to make cameos, which are used as brooches and as other types of jewelry. One layer of shell is chipped away to show another colored layer beneath. This cameo is of a Roman emperor. It was made nearly two thousand years ago.

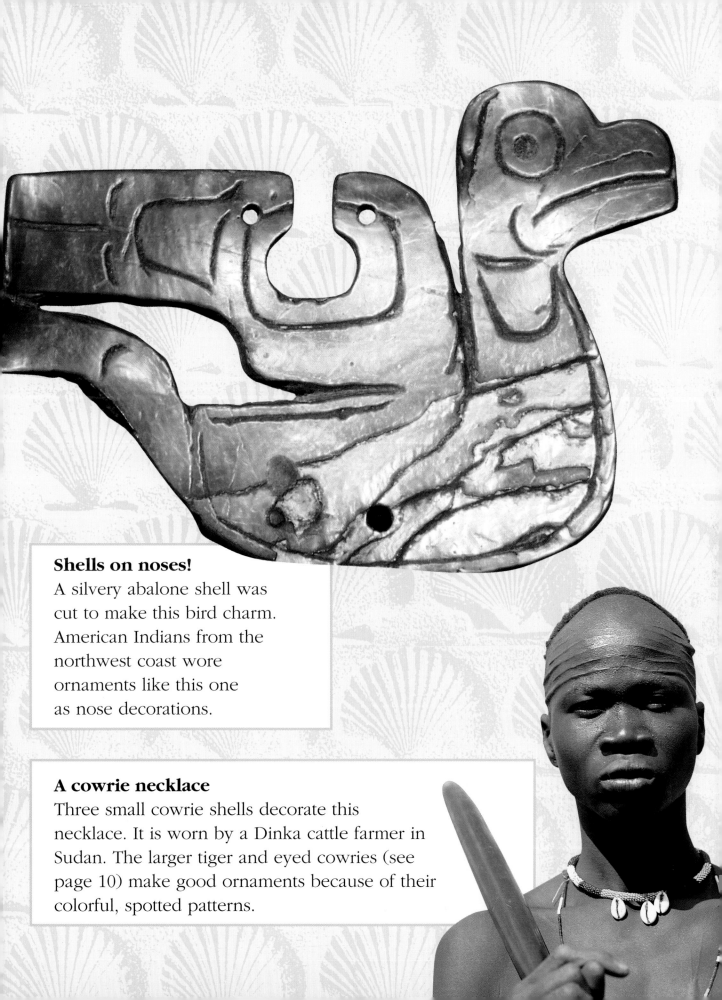

Shells on noses!

A silvery abalone shell was cut to make this bird charm. American Indians from the northwest coast wore ornaments like this one as nose decorations.

A cowrie necklace

Three small cowrie shells decorate this necklace. It is worn by a Dinka cattle farmer in Sudan. The larger tiger and eyed cowries (see page 10) make good ornaments because of their colorful, spotted patterns.

In Search of Pearls

If you open up an oyster's shell, you might find something special! Hard, shiny pearls are sometimes made inside.

Magic!
When sand or a tiny creature gets stuck underneath the shell of an oyster, the oyster makes shiny pearl layers around it.

Pearl farming
In Tahiti, oysters are farmed for their pearls. Most pearls are creamy white, but this oyster farm makes the rare, glossy, black ones.

Dangerous diving

These pearl divers are searching for oysters off the coast of Bahrain, in the Middle East. Pearl diving is very dangerous. But pearls found naturally in the ocean are much more valuable than those made on farms.

Pearls for a prince

Pearls have been prized all over the world for hundreds of years. Here you can see Shah Jehan, a famous Indian prince who lived over 400 years ago. He is decked with pearls. The one dangling from the middle necklace is called a drop pearl.

Shell Hills

Millions of years ago, huge numbers of shells and small skeletons were squashed down into chalk and limestone rock.

Limestone hills
Wind and rain have worn down this mass of limestone into low hills. People have cut into the hill to take out the stone at a place called a quarry. The limestone is used for building.

White horse

This famous landmark was cut into the chalk hills, called downs, in southern England. Only a thin layer of soil and grass covers chalk rock.

Chalk cliffs

Over thousands of years, the ocean has broken up and worn away some chalk hills to form cliffs. The cliffs show that some chalks are covered with whole fossil shells. Others, like these cliffs, contain cobbles and flints.

Gritty shells
Shell gravel is dug up in the Netherlands.

Crushed Shells

Millions of years ago, banks of crumbly shell gravel formed. Shell gravel contains a mineral called calcium. This is good for growing healthy crops and for raising healthy chickens!

Helping crops
Shell gravel is ground into a fine powder, called lime. This is spread over the soil to help crops grow better. Lime powder can also be made into toothpaste!

Eggshells!

Would you believe that chickens eat shells? The shells are crushed and added to their food. The calcium from the shells makes chickens' eggshells stronger.

Drawing with shells

Soft, white chalk is good for drawing with. People used to use it to draw on blackboards and slates. But the chalks we use in classrooms today are made from pressed slate powder. This contains the same mineral as chalk rock.

Looking for Oil

People look for oil near rock with a type of shell fossil in it. Over millions of years, the first tiny shells, plants, and animals were crushed into thick, black oil.

Shell oil
This oil worker in Nigeria works for the Shell Oil Company. The shell symbol shows the importance of shells to making oil.

Drilling for oil
Oil can be found under the seabed. Here, on the coast of Texas, an oil platform has been towed out to sea to drill for oil.

Oil for everyone

Crude oil is the name given to oil when it first comes out of the ground. Crude oil is treated or refined to make gas, petroleum, kerosene, diesel oil, and heavy oil. Oil is also used to make many other things, including plastic, dish detergent, and bubbles!

Dangerous oil

Oil is carried by tanker ships, pipelines, or trucks. If these crash or crack, oil leaks out. It covers land and floats on water. This seabird is soaked in oil from a spill. Amazingly, it is being cleaned using dish detergent, which is made from oil.

Shells for a Living

All over the world, people make a living out of shells. Shellfish are sold for food. Chalk and shell gravel are dug up. Oil spurts from hundreds of wells. With shells, we can make beautiful and useful things. But people need to be careful that there are plenty of shells to replace the ones that we use.

Mussel farming
Mussels cling to wooden posts on the coast of France, where they are farmed.

Shell seekers
Kogi Indians from Colombia comb the beach for shells. They will sell these to tourists and jewelry makers.

Lobsters for sale

What a huge lobster! A fish dealer is attracting customers with it in southwest Spain. Shellfish is a very popular type of food. More than two and a half million tons of mollusks alone are caught each year. Shellfish can sometimes carry germs from polluted waters. But they are treated with ultraviolet light to make them safe for people to eat.

Conch shells

Rainbow-colored conch shells are sold as ornaments in a market on one of the Bahama Islands.

Shell Crafts

Take a closer look at shells yourself
with some arts and crafts
activities. Here are some ideas
to help you get started.
If you can't find shells at a
beach, you can buy them in craft
stores or even at a fish dealer!

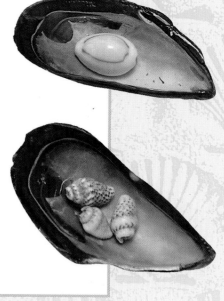

Shell shakers

Shells rattle a lot when they are shaken together.
They make an even better sound if you put
other shells inside of them. You can use mussel
shells, like these — cockle shells work well, too.

Split the shells into their two halves. Put
some small shells or oyster-shell grit in one half
(oyster-shell grit is used at the bottom of bird
cages and can be bought at pet stores). Smear
some glue around the edges. Lay the ribbon
near the pointed end of the shell. Put some glue
around the other half of the shell. Stick it firmly
on top. Leave it to set for about an hour.

Shell T-shirts

Brighten up an old, plain T-shirt for the summer, with some shell patterns. Use a shell that has ridges, like this scallop. Turn it on its textured side. Hold the material on top, and rub over it with fabric crayons. You can make a collage in the same way, using crayons on colored tissue paper, instead.

When you've finished with your scallop shell, you can use it to hold bath pearls or soap!

Unbeatable bubbles

Make a bubble-blowing mixture. Mix one teaspoon of dish detergent with 12 – 15 teaspoons of water. (Weak dish detergent uses 12 teaspoons of water, and strong detergent needs up to 15.)

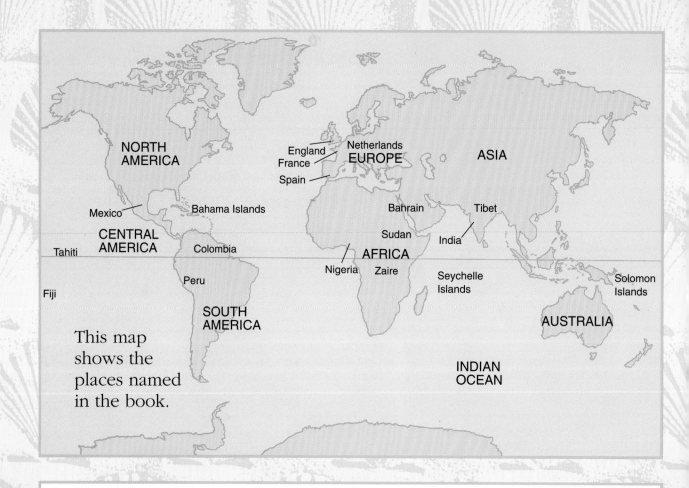

This map shows the places named in the book.

Further Reading

Benanti, Carol. *Seashells*. Random Books, 1994.

Lambert, David. *Seas and Oceans*. Raintree Steck-Vaughn, 1994.

Seashell Magic. Modern Curriculum Press, 1991.

Zoehfeld, Kathleen W. *A Shell Is Someone's Home*. HarperCollins, 1994.

Index

Acknowledgments
Editors: Rachel Cooke, Kathy DeVico
Design: Neil Sayer, Joyce Spicer
Production: Jenny Mulvanny, Scott Melcer
Photography: Michael Stannard (pages 28 & 29)
For permission to reproduce the following material, the author and publishers gratefully acknowledge the following:
Cover (top right) Michael Freeman/Bruce Coleman Ltd., (top left – a Sally lightfoot crab) Walter Rawlings/Robert Harding Picture Library, (bottom right) Werner Forman Archive/Provincial Museum, Victoria, British Columbia, Canada, (bottom left) C.B. & D.W. Frith/Bruce Coleman Ltd., (logo insert, front and back) J. Carmichael, Jr./The Image Bank **title page** (logo insert) J. Carmichael, Jr./The Image Bank, (main picture – mother of pearl inlay) L.C. Marigo/Bruce Coleman Ltd. **page 6** (top) Jeff Foott/Bruce Coleman Ltd., (bottom) Jane Burton/Bruce Coleman Ltd. **page 7** (top) Jane Burton/Bruce Coleman Ltd., (bottom) Jeff Foott/Bruce Coleman Ltd. **page 8** (top and bottom) Ronald Sheridan/The Ancient Art & Architecture Collection **page 9** (top) Mary Evans Picture Library, (bottom) Leslie Woodhead/The Hutchison Library **page 10** (top and center) The Bridgeman Art Library, (bottom) Andrew Hill/The Hutchison Library **page 11** (top) H.R. Dorig/Vision International/The Hutchison Library, (bottom) C.B. & D.W. Frith/Bruce Coleman Ltd. **page 12** (top) Ronald Sheridan/The Ancient Art & Architecture Collection, (bottom) Wood & Bull/The Image Bank **page 13** (top) Christine Osborne Pictures, (bottom) The Victoria & Albert Museum/Robert Harding Picture Library **page 14** (top) Werner Forman Archive/National Museum of Anthropology, Mexico, (bottom) Werner Forman Archive/The University Museum, Pennsylvania **page 15** (top) Anthony Cooper/ Ecoscene, (bottom) Werner Forman Archive **page 16** (top) Christine Osborne Pictures, (bottom) Ronald Sheridan/Ancient Art & Architecture Collection **page 17** (top) Werner Forman Archive/ Provincial Museum, Victoria, British Columbia, Canada, (bottom) The Hutchison Library **page 18** (top) Robin Constable/The Hutchison Library, (bottom) Ocean Images, Inc./The Image Bank **page 19** (top and center) The Hutchison Library, (bottom) Ronald Sheridan/The Ancient Art & Architecture Collection **page 20** Ayres/Ecoscene **page 21** (top) P.W. Hamilton/The Image Bank, (bottom) M.H. Black/Robert Harding Picture Library **page 22** (top) Anthony Cooper/ Ecoscene, (bottom) Sarah Errington/The Hutchison Library **page 23** (top) Robert Harding Picture Library, (center) Joe Devenney/The Image Bank, (bottom) The Hutchison Library **page 24** (top and bottom) Robert Harding Picture Library **page 25** (top) Michael Freeman/ Bruce Coleman Ltd., (bottom) Gryniewicz/Ecoscene **page 26** (top) Tordai/The Hutchison Library, (bottom) Nock/The Hutchison Library **page 27** (top) Wilkinson/Ecoscene, (bottom) Adrian Neville/Robert Harding Picture Library